Hal•Leonard

JAZZ PLAY-ALONG®

ok and CD for B♭, E♭, C and Bass Clef Instruments

Volume 109

Oscar Peterson

Arranged and Produced by
Mark Taylor and Jim Roberts

10 CLASSIC TUNES

BOOK

CD

ISBN 978-1-4234-7331-2

Hal•Leonard®
CORPORATION
7777 W. BLUEMOUND RD. P.O. BOX 13819 MILWAUKEE, WI 53213

Visit Hal Leonard Online at
www.halleonard.com

OSCAR PETERSON

Volume 109

Arranged and Produced by
Mark Taylor and Jim Roberts

Featured Players:

Graham Breedlove–Trumpet
John Desalme–Tenor Saxophone
Tony Nalker–Piano
Jim Roberts–Bass
Todd Harrison–Drums

**Recorded at Bias Studios, Springfield, Virginia
Bob Dawson, Engineer**

HOW TO USE THE CD:

Each song has <u>two</u> tracks:

1) Split Track/Melody

Woodwind, Brass, Keyboard, and **Mallet Players** can use this track as a learning tool for melody style and inflection.

Bass Players can learn and perform with this track – remove the recorded bass track by turning down the volume on the LEFT channel.

Keyboard and **Guitar Players** can learn and perform with this track – remove the recorded piano part by turning down the volume on the RIGHT channel.

2) Full Stereo Track

Soloists or **Groups** can learn and perform with this accompaniment track with the RHYTHM SECTION only.

BLUES FOR MARTHA

BY OSCAR PETERSON

C VERSION

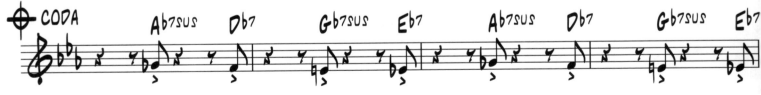

PLACE ST. HENRI

BY OSCAR PETERSON

C VERSION

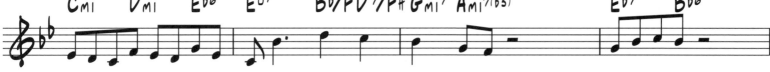

CAKEWALK

BY OSCAR PETERSON

C VERSION

SOLOS (3 CHORUSES)

HALLELUJAH TIME

BY OSCAR PETERSON

CD
5 : SPLIT TRACK/MELODY
6 : FULL STEREO TRACK

C VERSION

HYMN TO FREEDOM

BY OSCAR PETERSON

MOLTO RIT.

CD

C VERSION

LOVE BALLADE

BY OSCAR PETERSON

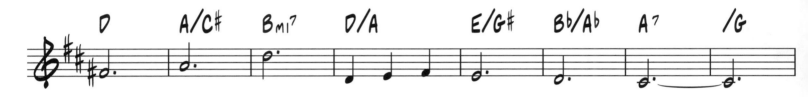

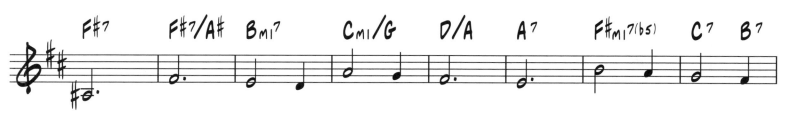

CD
11 : SPLIT TRACK/MELODY
12 : FULL STEREO TRACK

C VERSION

NIGERIAN MARKETPLACE

BY OSCAR PETERSON

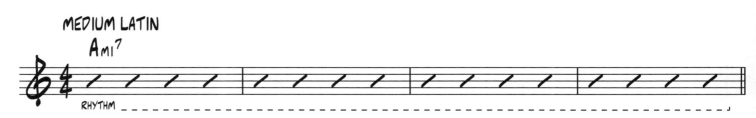

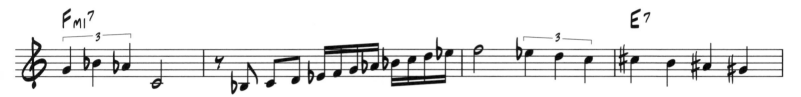

SOLOS (2 CHORUSES)

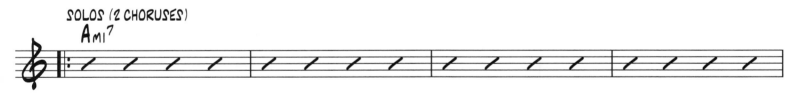

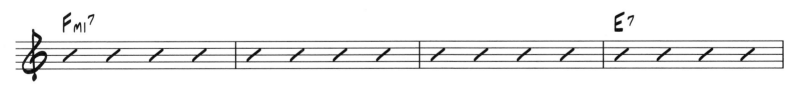

D.S. AL FINE
TAKE REPEAT

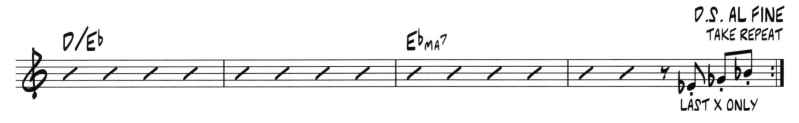

LAST X ONLY

CD

NOREEN'S NOCTURNE

BY OSCAR PETERSON

C VERSION

FAST SWING

CD

19 : SPLIT TRACK/MELODY
20 : FULL STEREO TRACK

TRUFFLES

BY OSCAR PETERSON

C VERSION

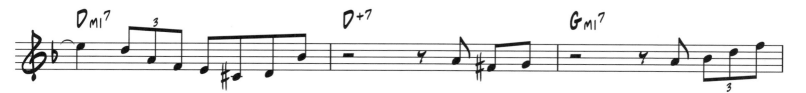

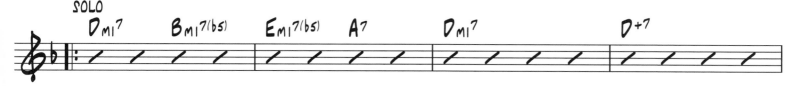

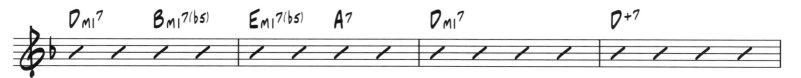

THE SMUDGE

BY OSCAR PETERSON

BLUES FOR MARTHA

BY OSCAR PETERSON

Bb VERSION

CD
❸ : SPLIT TRACK/MELODY
❹ : FULL STEREO TRACK

CAKEWALK

BY OSCAR PETERSON

Bb VERSION

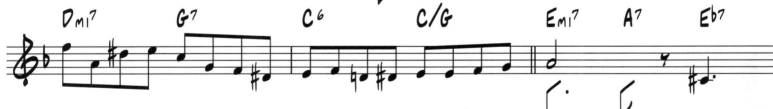

SOLOS (3 CHORUSES)

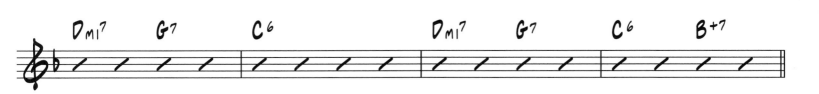

HALLELUJAH TIME

BY OSCAR PETERSON

HYMN TO FREEDOM

BY OSCAR PETERSON

Bb VERSION

CD

◆ 9: SPLIT TRACK/MELODY
◆ 10: FULL STEREO TRACK

LOVE BALLADE

BY OSCAR PETERSON

Bb VERSION

SLOW WALTZ

RIT.

NIGERIAN MARKETPLACE

BY OSCAR PETERSON

Bb VERSION

SOLOS (2 CHORUSES)

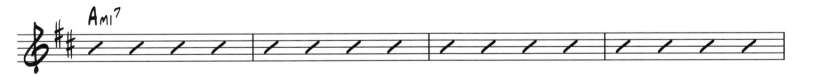

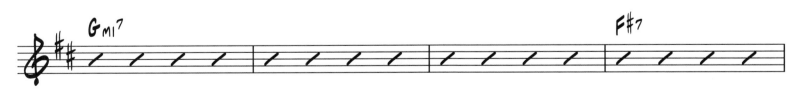

NOREEN'S NOCTURNE

BY OSCAR PETERSON

Bb VERSION

PLACE ST. HENRI

BY OSCAR PETERSON

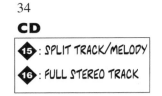

CD
15 : SPLIT TRACK/MELODY
16 : FULL STEREO TRACK

Bb VERSION

THE SMUDGE

BY OSCAR PETERSON

CD
17 : SPLIT TRACK/MELODY
18 : FULL STEREO TRACK

Bb VERSION

MEDIUM SWING

TRUFFLES

CD
- ◆19: SPLIT TRACK/MELODY
- ◆20: FULL STEREO TRACK

BY OSCAR PETERSON

Bb VERSION

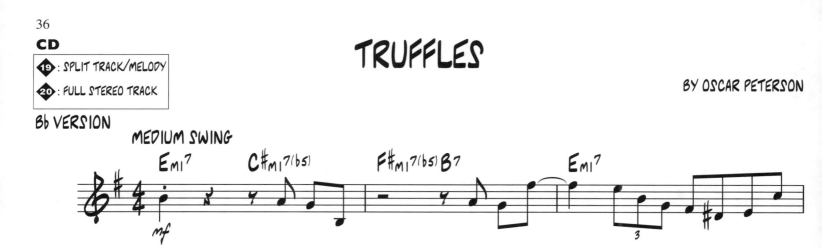

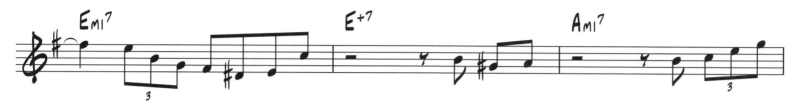

CD

① : SPLIT TRACK/MELODY
② : FULL STEREO TRACK

BLUES FOR MARTHA

BY OSCAR PETERSON

Eb VERSION

MEDIUM SWING

SOLOS (7 CHORUSES)

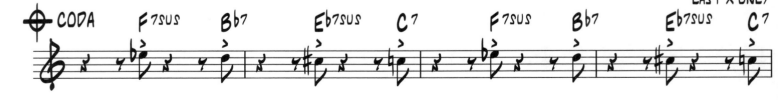

PLACE ST. HENRI

BY OSCAR PETERSON

Eb VERSION

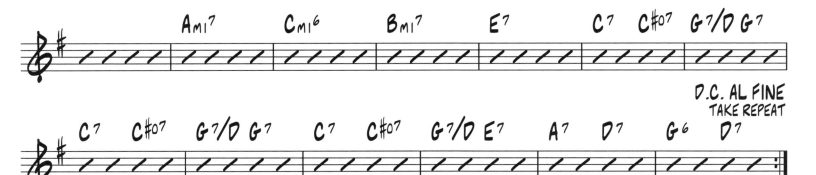

CAKEWALK

BY OSCAR PETERSON

Eb VERSION

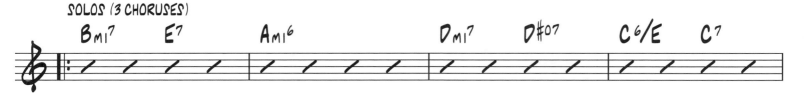

SOLOS (3 CHORUSES)

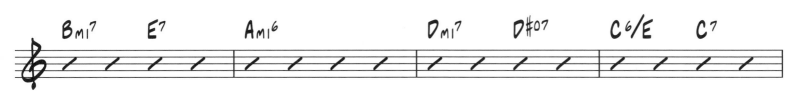

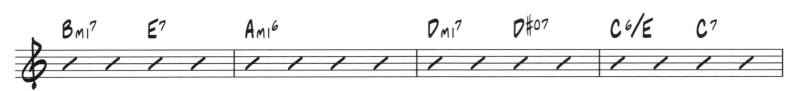

HALLELUJAH TIME

BY OSCAR PETERSON

Eb VERSION

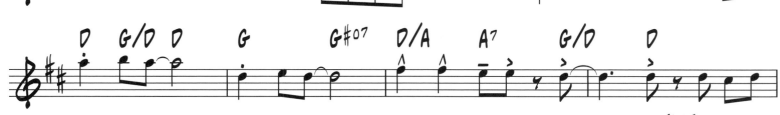

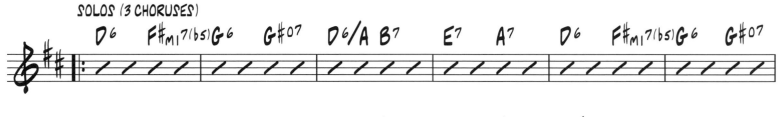

SOLOS (3 CHORUSES)

HYMN TO FREEDOM

BY OSCAR PETERSON

Eb VERSION

LOVE BALLADE

BY OSCAR PETERSON

Eb VERSION

SLOW WALTZ

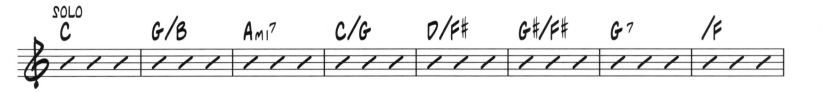

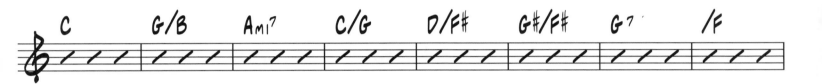

NIGERIAN MARKETPLACE

BY OSCAR PETERSON

Eb VERSION

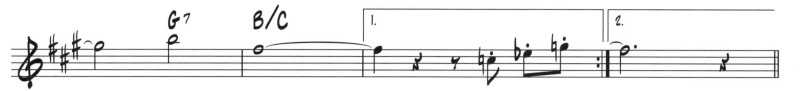

SOLOS (2 CHORUSES)

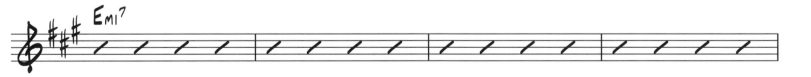

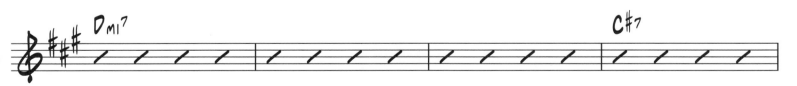

NOREEN'S NOCTURNE

BY OSCAR PETERSON

Eb VERSION

E♭/C Fmi7(♭5)/B C C/B♭ Ami7 Dmi7(♭5)/G♯ G7sus G7
SOLO BREAK
SOLOS
C6 E7/B Ami C7/G F6 E7 Ami C7/G F6 F♯o7 C6/G A7
Dmi7 G7 C6 E7/B Ami C7/G F6 E7 Ami C7/G
F6 F♯o7 C6/G A7 Dmi7 G7 C6 E7 Ami E7
Ami D7 G6 Ami7 D7 Dmi7 G7 C6 E7/B Ami C7/G
F6 E7 Ami C7/G F6 F♯o7 C6/G A7 Dmi7 G7 C6
Cma7 Bmi7 E7 Ami7 Gmi7 C7 Fma7 F♯mi7 B7 Emi7 A7
F6 E+7 E♭7 D7 C♯ma7
SOLO
E7 Ami E7 Ami D7 G6 Ami7 D7 Dmi7 G7
Cma7 Bmi7 E7 Ami7 Gmi7 C7 Fma7 F♯mi7 B7 Emi7 A7
F6 E+7 E♭7 D7 C♯ma7 Cma7

TRUFFLES

CD
◆19◆: SPLIT TRACK/MELODY
◆20◆: FULL STEREO TRACK

BY OSCAR PETERSON

Eb VERSION

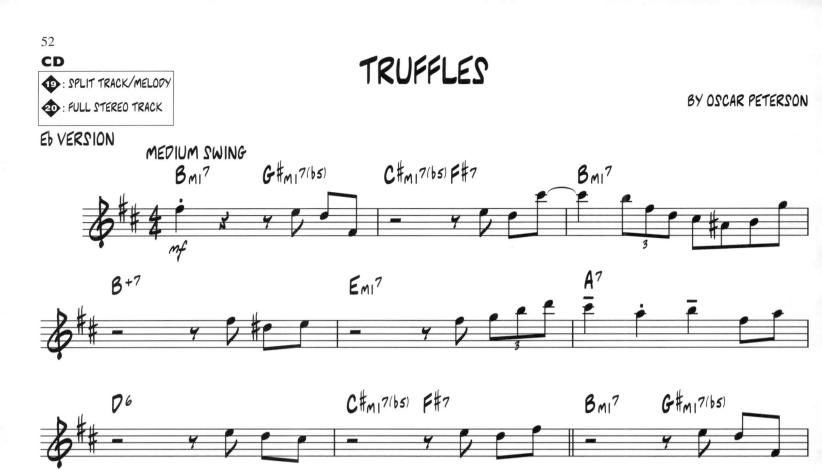

THE SMUDGE

BY OSCAR PETERSON

BLUES FOR MARTHA

BY OSCAR PETERSON

𝄢: C VERSION

MEDIUM SWING

CAKEWALK

BY OSCAR PETERSON

SOLOS (3 CHORUSES)

HALLELUJAH TIME

BY OSCAR PETERSON

HYMN TO FREEDOM

BY OSCAR PETERSON

𝄢: C VERSION

CD

9 : SPLIT TRACK/MELODY
10 : FULL STEREO TRACK

LOVE BALLADE

BY OSCAR PETERSON

🎼: C VERSION

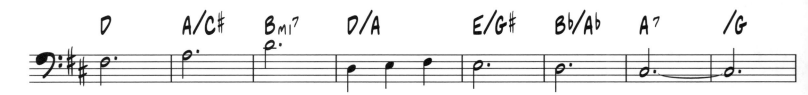

NIGERIAN MARKETPLACE

BY OSCAR PETERSON

𝄢: C VERSION

FINE

SOLOS (2 CHORUSES)

D.S. AL FINE
TAKE REPEAT

LAST X ONLY

NOREEN'S NOCTURNE

BY OSCAR PETERSON

𝄢: C VERSION

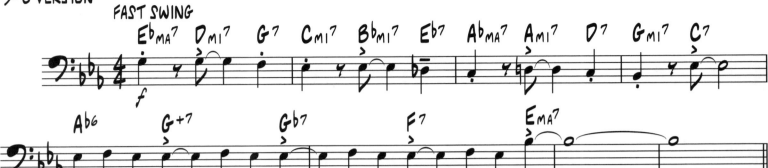

SOLO BREAK

Gb/Eb Abmi7(b5)/D Eb   Eb/Db Cmi7 Fmi7(b5)/B Bb7sus   Bb7

SOLOS
Eb6   G7/D Cmi   Eb7/Bb Ab6   G7   Cmi   Eb7/Bb Ab6   A°7   Eb6/Bb C7

Fmi7   Bb7   Eb6   G7/D Cmi   Eb7/Bb Ab6   G7   Cmi   Eb7/Bb

Ab6 A°7 Eb6/Bb C7   Fmi7 Bb7 Eb6   G7   Cmi   G7

Cmi   F7   Bb6   Cmi7 F7 Fmi7 Bb7 Eb6 G7/D Cmi   Eb7/Bb

Ab6 G7   Cmi   Eb7/Bb Ab6 A°7   Eb6/Bb C7   Fmi7 Bb7 Eb6

EbMA7 Dmi7 G7 Cmi7 Bbmi7 Eb7 AbMA7 Ami7 D7 Gmi7 C7

Ab6   G+7   Gb7   F7   EMA7

SOLO
G7   Cmi   G7   Cmi   F7   Bb6   Cmi7 F7 Fmi7 Bb7

EbMA7 Dmi7 G7 Cmi7 Bbmi7 Eb7 AbMA7 Ami7 D7 Gmi7 C7

Ab6   G+7   Gb7   F7   EMA7   EbMA7

CD
15: SPLIT TRACK/MELODY
16: FULL STEREO TRACK

PLACE ST. HENRI

BY OSCAR PETERSON

𝄢 C VERSION

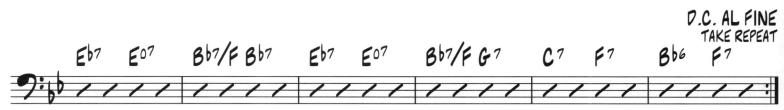

THE SMUDGE

BY OSCAR PETERSON

CD

19 : SPLIT TRACK/MELODY
20 : FULL STEREO TRACK

TRUFFLES

BY OSCAR PETERSON

𝄢: C VERSION

Presenting the Hal Leonard JAZZ PLAY-ALONG SERIES

1. DUKE ELLINGTON
00841644 .... $16.95

2. MILES DAVIS
00841645 .... $16.95

3. THE BLUES
00841646 .... $16.99

4. JAZZ BALLADS
00841691 .... $16.99

5. BEST OF BEBOP
00841689 .... $16.99

6. JAZZ CLASSICS WITH EASY CHANGES
00841690 .... $16.99

7. ESSENTIAL JAZZ STANDARDS
00843000 .... $16.99

8. ANTONIO CARLOS JOBIM AND THE ART OF THE BOSSA NOVA
00843001 .... $16.95

9. DIZZY GILLESPIE
00843002 .... $16.99

10. DISNEY CLASSICS
00843003 .... $16.99

11. RODGERS AND HART – FAVORITES
00843004 .... $16.99

12. ESSENTIAL JAZZ CLASSICS
00843005 .... $16.99

13. JOHN COLTRANE
00843006 .... $16.95

14. IRVING BERLIN
00843007 .... $15.99

15. RODGERS & HAMMERSTEIN
00843008 .... $15.99

16. COLE PORTER
00843009 .... $15.95

17. COUNT BASIE
00843010 .... $16.95

18. HAROLD ARLEN
00843011 .... $15.95

19. COOL JAZZ
00843012 .... $15.95

20. CHRISTMAS CAROLS
00843080 .... $14.95

21. RODGERS AND HART – CLASSICS
00843014 .... $14.95

22. WAYNE SHORTER
00843015 .... $16.95

23. LATIN JAZZ
00843016 .... $16.95

24. EARLY JAZZ STANDARDS
00843017 .... $14.95

25. CHRISTMAS JAZZ
00843018 .... $16.95

26. CHARLIE PARKER
00843019 .... $16.95

27. GREAT JAZZ STANDARDS
00843020 .... $15.99

28. BIG BAND ERA
00843021 .... $15.99

29. LENNON AND McCARTNEY
00843022 .... $16.95

30. BLUES' BEST
00843023 .... $15.99

31. JAZZ IN THREE
00843024 .... $15.99

32. BEST OF SWING
00843025 .... $15.99

33. SONNY ROLLINS
00843029 .... $15.95

34. ALL TIME STANDARDS
00843030 .... $15.99

35. BLUESY JAZZ
00843031 .... $15.99

36. HORACE SILVER
00843032 .... $16.99

37. BILL EVANS
00843033 .... $16.95

38. YULETIDE JAZZ
00843034 .... $16.95

39. "ALL THE THINGS YOU ARE" & MORE JEROME KERN SONGS
00843035 .... $15.99

40. BOSSA NOVA
00843036 .... $15.99

41. CLASSIC DUKE ELLINGTON
00843037 .... $16.99

42. GERRY MULLIGAN – FAVORITES
00843038 .... $16.99

43. GERRY MULLIGAN – CLASSICS
00843039 .... $16.95

44. OLIVER NELSON
00843040 .... $16.95

45. JAZZ AT THE MOVIES
00843041 .... $15.99

46. BROADWAY JAZZ STANDARDS
00843042 .... $15.99

47. CLASSIC JAZZ BALLADS
00843043 .... $15.99

48. BEBOP CLASSICS
00843044 .... $16.99

49. MILES DAVIS – STANDARDS
00843045 .... $16.95

50. GREAT JAZZ CLASSICS
00843046 .... $15.99

51. UP-TEMPO JAZZ
00843047 .... $15.99

52. STEVIE WONDER
00843048 .... $15.95

53. RHYTHM CHANGES
00843049 .... $15.99

54. "MOONLIGHT IN VERMONT" & OTHER GREAT STANDARDS
00843050 .... $15.99

55. BENNY GOLSON
00843052 .... $15.95

56. "GEORGIA ON MY MIND" & OTHER SONGS BY HOAGY CARMICHAEL
00843056 .... $15.99

57. VINCE GUARALDI
00843057 .... $16.99

58. MORE LENNON AND McCARTNEY
00843059 .... $15.99

59. SOUL JAZZ
00843060 .... $15.99

60. DEXTER GORDON
00843061 .... $15.95

61. MONGO SANTAMARIA
00843062 .... $15.95

62. JAZZ-ROCK FUSION
00843063 .... $14.95

63. CLASSICAL JAZZ
00843064 .... $14.95

64. TV TUNES
00843065 .... $14.95

65. SMOOTH JAZZ
00843066 .... $16.99

66. A CHARLIE BROWN CHRISTMAS
00843067 .... $16.99

67. CHICK COREA
00843068 .... $15.95

68. CHARLES MINGUS
00843069 .... $16.95

69. CLASSIC JAZZ
00843071 .... $15.99

70. THE DOORS
00843072 .... $14.95

71. COLE PORTER CLASSICS
00843073 .... $14.95

72. CLASSIC JAZZ BALLADS
00843074 .... $15.99

73. JAZZ/BLUES
00843075 .... $14.95

74. BEST JAZZ CLASSICS
00843076 .... $15.99

75. PAUL DESMOND
00843077 .... $14.95

76. BROADWAY JAZZ BALLADS
00843078 .... $15.99

77. JAZZ ON BROADWAY
00843079 .... $15.99

78. STEELY DAN
00843070 .... $14.99

79. MILES DAVIS – CLASSICS
00843081 .... $15.99

80. JIMI HENDRIX
00843083 .... $15.99

81. FRANK SINATRA – CLASSICS
00843084 .... $15.99

82. FRANK SINATRA – STANDARDS
00843085 .... $15.99

83. ANDREW LLOYD WEBBER
00843104 .... $14.95

84. BOSSA NOVA CLASSICS
00843105 .... $14.95

85. MOTOWN HITS
00843109 .... $14.95

86. BENNY GOODMAN
00843110 .... $14.95

87. DIXIELAND
00843111 .... $14.95

88. DUKE ELLINGTON FAVORITES
00843112 .... $14.95

89. IRVING BERLIN FAVORITES
00843113 .... $14.95

90. THELONIOUS MONK CLASSICS
00841262 .... $16.99

91. THELONIOUS MONK FAVORITES
00841263 .... $16.99

92. LEONARD BERNSTEIN
00450134 .... $14.99

93. DISNEY FAVORITES
00843142 .... $14.99

94. RAY
00843143 .... $14.95

95. JAZZ AT THE LOUNGE
00843144 .... $14.99

96. LATIN JAZZ STANDARDS
00843145 .... $14.99

97. MAYBE I'M AMAZED
00843148 .... $14.99

98. DAVE FRISHBERG
00843149 .... $15.99

99. SWINGING STANDARDS
00843150 .... $14.99

100. LOUIS ARMSTRONG
00740423 .... $15.99

101. BUD POWELL
00843152 .... $14.99

102. JAZZ POP
00843153 .... $14.99

103. ON GREEN DOLPHIN STREET & OTHER JAZZ CLASSICS
00843154 .... $14.99

104. ELTON JOHN
00843155 .... $14.99

105. SOULFUL JAZZ
00843151 .... $14.99

106. SLO' JAZZ
00843117 .... $14.99

107. MOTOWN CLASSICS
00843116 .... $14.99

111. COOL CHRISTMAS
00843162 .... $15.99